Shadows Inside:

Exploring the Deepness of Depression

By

PAUL T. KAAN

Shawdow inside

Table of Contents

Shawdow inside

Conclusion:

Introduction:

In the tranquil corners of the psyche, where shadows wait and feelings back and forth movement, lies a scene natural to many but not yet figured out by many. This is the domain of melancholy, a complex and nuanced experience that rises above its clinical definition. Welcome to "Shadows Inside: Exploring the Deepness of Depression," an excursion into the core of this frequently misconstrued, yet significantly effective, feature of the human condition.

Melancholy, similar to the shadows that protrude in the blurring light, can project its presence across each part of life. It opposes straightforward arrangements, winding through the woven artwork of our science, brain research, and climate. As we set out on this investigation, we welcome you to throw away predispositions and enter a space where the language of feeling becomes the overwhelming focus.

In the principal parts, we will strip back the layers, looking at the signs that signal the beginning of this inside storm. What's the significance here to convey the heaviness of shadows? How can one explore the undetectable fight that rages inside? We'll look for replies to these inquiries, perceiving that the excursion into the profundities of sadness is both individual and general.

Our endeavor will take us through the complicated strings that structure the mind-boggling embroidery of despondency. Natural elements, mental aspects, and ecological impacts—

Shawdow inside

each string adds to the texture of this baffling experience.
Through understanding the complexities, we expect to
enlighten the scene, dissipate misinterpretations, and
encourage humane mindfulness.

As we progress, we'll give voice to the quiet battles that
frequently unfold in secret. Individual accounts, imparted
through fortitude and weakness, will reverberate through these
pages. These are the tales that overcome any issues among
disconnection and association, showing the way that in our
common human experience, understanding can thrive.

In the sections that follow, we'll investigate ways of exploring
the dimness. From survival strategies to restorative
methodologies and way of life changes, there are roads that
lead towards the light. However, in doing so, we defy the
unavoidable shame that covers sadness. Fantasies and
confusions should be disentangled, accounting for compassion
and understanding.

No investigation of sadness would be finished without
recognizing the job of connections and the local area. Secures
in the tempest, they offer comfort and backing. Through the
voices of the individuals who have navigated the profundities,
we'll find out about the flexibility that can rise up out of
difficulty, giving motivation to those actually tracking down
their direction.

This book isn't simply a work about the difficulties presented
by wretchedness; it is a manual for recuperation. In the
closing sections, we'll explore the way to recuperate,

Shawdow inside

underscoring the significance of looking for proficient
assistance and embracing a comprehensive methodology that
envelops the psyche, body, and soul.
Our process ends with a reflection on developing mental
prosperity. What are the procedures for taking care of oneself
that can strengthen the soul? How might we forestall the
repetition of the shadows that once took steps to overwhelm
us? Through these experiences, we'll embrace trust as a steady
friend on the consistently developing excursion toward a more
brilliant tomorrow.
As we set out together into the core of "Shadows Inside," may
these pages act as both a lamp to enlighten the way and an
ally for the people who walk it.

Section 1

Defining Depression: Navigating the Emotional Labyrinth

Depression is a perplexing and diverse psychological well-being condition that significantly influences a person's considerations, feelings, and, generally speaking, prosperity. It goes past intermittent sensations of bitterness or brief close-to-home lows, developing into an industrious and inescapable expression that can influence everyday working and personal satisfaction.

Key Characteristics of Depression:

1. Tireless Pity and Loss of Interest:
Melancholy is, in many cases, portrayed by an unavoidable feeling of bitterness or void that endures for a lengthy period. A striking element is the decreased interest or delight in exercises that were once pleasant.

2. Changes in Rest Examples:
Aggravations at rest are normal in the depression. This can appear as sleep deprivation, where people battle to fall or stay unconscious, or hypersomnia, including unnecessary tiredness.

3. Weakness and Low Energy:

Shawdow inside

People encountering Depression frequently report industrious weakness, even after insignificant physical or mental effort. Low energy levels add to a feeling of dormancy and inactivity.

4. Trouble Thinking and Deciding:
Discouragement can affect mental capabilities, prompting troubles in focus, navigation, and memory. Errands that once appeared to be reasonable may become overpowering.

5. Sensations of Uselessness or Responsibility:
Pessimistic self-insight is a typical part of wretchedness, with people frequently encountering sensations of uselessness, responsibility, or self-fault. These feelings add to a reduced sense of identity.

6. Changes in Craving or Weight:
Massive changes in hunger, prompting weight reduction or gain, are characteristic of sorrow. Some might encounter a decline in cravings, while others might go to nourishment for solace.

7. Rest. Unsettling influences:
Depression can disturb the regular rest-wake cycle, prompting sleep deprivation or hypersomnia. Rest and unsettling influences add to a feeling of weariness and, generally speaking, prosperity.

8. Actual side effects:
Notwithstanding profound and mental angles, wretchedness can appear in actual side effects. These may include

Shawdow inside

migraines, stomach-related issues, and summed-up torment, further affecting a person's general wellbeing.

It's urgent to perceive that the downturn is a heterogeneous condition, implying that its show can change broadly among people. The seriousness of side effects, the term of episodes, and the particular blend of close-to-home and actual appearances add to the intricacy of characterizing and grasping sorrow.

While this outline gives an overall system, it's essential to take note that a downturn is a nuanced and individual experience. Finding and successful administration frequently include an exhaustive evaluation by emotional wellness experts who consider an individual's extraordinary conditions and design mediations as needed.

The Weight of Shadows: Navigating the Burden of Depression

The figurative weight of shadows with regards to depression epitomizes the significant weight that people conveying this emotional wellness challenge frequently experience. These shadows are not simple transient obscurity but rather steady, weighty buddies that cast a pall over different parts of life.

1. Close-to-home weight:

The profound weight of depression is much the same as conveying a weighty heap of misery, despair, and, frequently, a mind-boggling feeling of sadness. These feelings can be

Shawdow inside

sweeping, influencing one's capacity to track down satisfaction or even imagine a more promising time to come.

2. Social Separation:

Depression creates shaded areas in friendly associations, adding to a feeling of disengagement. The heaviness of these shadows makes them try to draw in with others, encouraging an unavoidable sensation of being misjudged or disengaged.

3. Mental strain:

The shadows of misery stretch out to mental domains, where the weight appears as hardships in focus, memory, and navigation. Errands that were once standard might become exhausting under this mental type of depression.

4. Actual Effect:

The heaviness of shadows isn't bound to the profound and mental domains; it saturates the actual area. Weariness, dormancy, and disturbed rest designs add to the actual cost, further escalating the weight.

5. Self-Insight:

Wretchedness frequently contorts self-insight, adding a weight of pessimistic self-talk and serious insecurities. The heaviness of these shadows can dissolve confidence, making it difficult to remember one's own value.

6. Everyday Working:

The shadows of misery cast a pall over day-to-day exercises. Basic errands can feel like amazing difficulties, and the

Shawdow inside

heaviness of shadows prevents the capacity to explore day-to-day existence without sweat that others might underestimate.

7. Sadness:

Maybe the heaviest load on everything is the feeling of sadness that goes with discouragement. The shadows darken the chance of progress, making it hard to imagine a future liberated from the weight they force.

Perceiving and tending to the heaviness of shadows is a pivotal part of exploring the intricacies of melancholy. Proficient help, understanding from friends and family, and taking care of oneself act as fundamental apparatuses for lifting this weight and carrying light into the shadows. The excursion towards reducing the weight of despondency is a slow cycle, and each step taken towards looking for help and encouraging versatility adds to the continuous dispersal of these weighty shadows.

Section 2

Embarking on the Journey: Recognizing the Shadows

In the maze of the human experience, there exists a way less taken, an excursion through the complexities of the psyche where shadows stretch and feelings take on a significant weight. This is the odyssey of melancholy, a journey not generally embraced by decision, yet one that many end up exploring. As we leave on this campaign into the domains of "Shadows Inside: Exploring the Deepness of Depression," we are going up against the basic undertaking of perceiving the signs that mark the entry to this complex excursion.

The beginning of misery is frequently unpretentious—murmurs in the breeze as opposed to loud announcements. It appears in the tranquil minutes when the shades of life appear to blur and the dynamic quality of presence is supplanted by a ghostly quietness. To leave on this excursion is to recognize the presence of these shadows, to perceive the unpretentious changes in profound scenes that envoy the start of an inner odyssey.

As we dig into the principal parts, it becomes obvious that downturn, similar to a talented illusionist, can shroud itself in different pretenses. It could take on the appearance of steady pity, unrelenting exhaustion, or a separation from the world. Perceiving these signs requires a sharp sense of mindfulness

Shawdow inside

and the capacity to figure out the deeper, hidden meaning of one's own close-to-home story.

The undetectable fight that goes with the excursion into depression is maybe the most overwhelming. It's a fight battled not on far-off landmarks but rather inside the openings of the brain. The weapons are not swords and safeguards but rather the versatility of the soul and the mental fortitude to face one's own weaknesses. To set out on this excursion is to face the mystery of an imperceptible battle that leaves permanent imprints on the spirit.

However, in perceiving the shadows and recognizing the fight inside, there is an essential snapshot of strengthening. It is the second when the excursion changes from a compulsory plunge into the void to a cognizant work to explore the intricate landscape of feelings. This acknowledgment turns into the compass that directs the explorer through the exciting bends in the road of the maze.

In "Shadows Inside," we welcome you to go along with us on this endeavor as spectators as well as individual voyagers. The way might be testing, and the shadows may on occasion appear to be overpowering; however, the demonstration of setting out on this excursion is, in itself, an attestation of flexibility. As we push ahead, let us clutch the comprehension that perceiving the shadows is the most important move toward uncovering them.

Recognizing the Signs: Illuminating the Shadows of Depression

Perceiving the indications of depression is significant for early mediation and support. While the experience of sorrow can shift broadly among people, certain normal markers might suggest the presence of this emotional wellness challenge. Here are key signs to be aware of:

1. Determined Pity:
an overarching and delayed feeling of pity or vacancy that doesn't lift, impacting one's general state of mind and point of view.

2. Loss of Interest or Joy:
reduced interest or delight in exercises that were once charming, joined by a general feeling of lack of care towards life's interests.

3. Changes in Rest Examples:
disturbances in rest, like a sleeping disorder or hypersomnia, where people might battle to rest or experience exorbitant lethargy.

4. Weariness and low energy:
persistent weariness and low energy levels, regardless of how much rest is acquired.

5. Trouble concentrating:

Shawdow inside

challenges in keeping up with center, simply deciding, and
focusing on errands, prompting a decrease in mental working.

6. Sensations of Uselessness or Responsibility:
continuous and extreme sensations of uselessness,
responsibility, or self-fault, adding to a negative sense of self-
insight.

7. Changes in Craving or Weight:
massive changes in hunger, bringing about recognizable
weight reduction or gain over a somewhat brief period.

8. Crabbiness or Fretfulness:
expanded crabbiness, fretfulness, or sensations of fomentation
that are not regular for the person.

9. Actual side effects:
the development of actual side effects like migraines,
stomach-related issues, or unexplained torment, frequently
without a reasonable actual reason.

10. Social Withdrawal:
withdrawal from social exercises, segregation from loved
ones, and a hesitance to take part in friendly cooperation.

11. Contemplations of Death or Self-Destructive Ideation:
Relentless considerations of death, biting the dust, or self-
destructive ideation Any sign of self-destructive
contemplation requires prompt consideration and expert
intercession.

Shawdow inside

It's essential to take note that encountering at least one of these signs isn't guaranteed to affirm misery. A conclusion ought to be made by a certified medical care professional in view of a thorough evaluation of side effects, their terms, and their effect on everyday working.
On the off chance that you or somebody you know is showing indications of despondency, it is pivotal to look for proficient assistance. Emotional well-being experts can give a precise determination, offer custom-made treatment choices, and support people in exploring
the excursion towards recuperating.

The Invisible Battle: Confronting Depression's Hidden Struggles

Depression wages an invisible battle, its effect disguised underneath grins, regular schedules, and social communications. This quiet battle unfurls inside the intricacies of the psyche and feelings, frequently leaving no apparent scars except for impacting each feature of a person's life.

1. Inconspicuous Personal Disturbance:
Behind an apparently made outside, people engaging in despondency wrestle with serious personal unrest—sensations of bitterness, sadness, and depression that stay stowed away from relaxed perception.

2. The Cover of Predictability:

Shawdow inside

The undetectable fight prompts people to wear a veil of predictability, hiding the internal conflict to adjust to cultural assumptions. The capacity to explore day-to-day existence can create a veneer that veils the significant difficulties inside.

3. Disengagement in a Packed Room:
Depression breeds a feeling of separation, even amidst parties. The imperceptible fight unfolds as people battle to interface with others; their conflicts, under the surface, take cover behind a shroud of social cooperation.

4. Grins That Cover the Shadows:
Grins can turn into a cover, concealing the shadows of misery. People might seem happy while grappling with a profound weight, making a distinct difference between the noticeable and imperceptible parts of their experience.

5. Quiet shouts:
The fight against despondency frequently includes quiet shouts for help—inward cries that go unheard. People might connect quietly or pull out of themselves, endeavoring to impart the undetectable aggravation they bear.

6. The Heaviness of Implicit Words:
In the undetectable fight, words frequently go implicit. Communicating the profundity of profound torment turns into a test, leaving others ignorant about the quiet battles being pursued inside the singular's psyche.

7. Day-to-day wins: hiding inward battles

Shawdow inside

Day-to day achievements, regardless of how little, can cover the inward fights people face. Accomplishments might coincide with stowed-away battles, making a Catch-22 between outward achievement and internal conflict.

8. Capricious Changes:
The undetectable fight is set apart by capricious vacillations in temperament and energy. People might explore snapshots of evident predictability, only to be maneuvered once more into the shadows of misery abruptly.

Perceiving and recognizing the undetectable fight is a critical stage in cultivating understanding and backing for those wrestling with melancholy. While the scars may not be apparent, the effect is significant. It stresses the significance of developing sympathy, giving a place of refuge to open discourse, and looking for proficient help to address the secret battles inside the imperceptible fight against depression.

Section 3

The Complex Tapestry: Unraveling the Threads of Depression

In the complicated winding of human life, strings of intricacy entwine, making an embroidery that is remarkably our own. However, inside this embroidery, there are strings of an alternate tone, strings that structure the many-sided examples of depression. As we proceed with our investigation into the profundities of "Shadows Inside: Exploring the Deepness of Depression ," it is fundamental to disentangle these strings and figure out the complex idea of melancholy that colors the texture of our lives.

The main string, woven into the actual center of our being, is natural. It discusses synapses moving in fragile balance and hereditary inclinations that cast shadows across ages. To appreciate sadness is to dig into the domain of science, perceiving that the mind, that multifaceted organ, holds both the keys to understanding and the secrets of weakness.

However, the embroidered artwork doesn't stop at science. It stretches out into the openings of the brain, into the second string of mental aspects. Here, contemplations become the loom, winding around examples of cognizance and insight. Depression murmurs in twisted self-discernments and the tireless reiteration of negative considerations. Disentangling this string requires a nuanced investigation of the mind,

Shawdow inside

recognizing the interconnectedness of contemplations and feelings.

As we explore further into the mind-boggling embroidery, we experience the third string: natural impacts. The environmental factors where we reside, the connections we fashion, and the cultural designs that shape every one of us add to the texture of despondency. It is a many-sided dance among nature and sustainment, where outer elements entwine with inner weaknesses. Understanding this string requires an assessment of the more extensive setting where the singular exists.

To unwind these strings is to bring lucidity to the intricacy of sorrow. It is an affirmation that the embroidery isn't woven from a solitary strand yet is a union of different components, each having its own impact on the orchestra of the human experience. The test lies in seeing each string separately as well as in knowing the harmonies and discords that emerge when they meet.

In "Shadows Inside," we welcome you to go with us as we cautiously disentangle these strings, looking at the natural, mental, and ecological features of melancholy. Thusly, we desire to reveal insight into the many-sided designs that arise, encouraging a more profound comprehension of the embroidery that shapes the encounters of those exploring the intricacies of wretchedness.

Biological Factors in Depression: Unraveling the Neurochemical Tapestry

Depression, in its complicated embroidery, is impacted by various organic factors that add to its beginning, movement, and appearance. Understanding these natural underpinnings gives knowledge into the intricacy of this psychological wellness condition.

1. Synapse Awkward nature:
One of the vital organic elements in sadness includes irregular characteristics in synapses, the substance couriers that communicate signals between nerve cells. Diminished degrees of serotonin, norepinephrine, and dopamine are ordinarily connected with burdensome side effects.

2. Cerebrum Construction and Capability:
Primary and useful changes in the mind assume a significant role in discouragement. Adjustments in regions like the hippocampus, amygdala, and prefrontal cortex have been noticed. These progressions influence state-of-mind guidelines, close-to-home reactions, and mental capabilities.

3. Hereditary Inclination:
Hereditary elements contribute essentially to the weakness of sadness. People with a family background of sorrow are at an expanded gamble, proposing a genetic part. Explicit hereditary varieties might impact weakness and burdensome problems.

4. Hormonal Impacts:
Hormonal variances, especially those corresponding to the endocrine framework, can add to sorrow. Changes in cortisol levels, the pressure chemical, have been connected to burdensome side effects. Also, hormonal movements during pubescence, pregnancy, and menopause can influence temperament.

5. Irritation and Insusceptible Framework Dysregulation:
Ongoing irritation and dysregulation of the resistant framework have been ensnared in depression. The exchange between provocative cycles and the focal sensory system can add to the turn of events and worsen burdensome side effects.

6. Neuroendocrine Elements:
The connection between the apprehensive and endocrine frameworks, known as the neuroendocrine framework, plays a part in sorrow. Dysregulation of chemicals created by the nerve center, pituitary organ, and adrenal organs can add to burdensome side effects.

7. Organic Clock Disturbances:
Disturbances in circadian rhythms, the body's interior clock controlling rest and wake cycles, can add to burdensome issues. Sporadic rest examples and aggravations in the rest-wake cycle are normal highlights of discouragement.

8. Epigenetic Changes:
Epigenetic factors, which include alterations to quality articulation without changing the hidden DNA arrangement, can impact defenselessness to despondency. Ecological

variables and educational encounters can contribute to epigenetic changes that influence emotional wellness.

It's essential to take note that these organic factors frequently connect with natural and psychosocial impacts, creating a complicated transaction that adds to the beginning and course of misery. The all-encompassing comprehension of discouragement consolidates the unpredictable associations between science, brain research, and the climate, directing extensive ways to deal with finding and treatment.

Psychological Dimensions of Depression: Unraveling the Inner Landscape

Depression stretches out past its natural roots to envelop a rich embroidery of mental aspects. Understanding these aspects is fundamental for an exhaustive understanding of the many-sided exchange between the psyche and feelings and the improvement of burdensome side effects.

1. Mental Examples:
Contorted thought designs are normal in sadness, including negative translations of oneself, the world, and what's to come. Mental contortions add to a negative perspective and can propagate sensations of sadness.

2. Profound Guidelines:
Trouble controlling feelings is the key to discouragement. People might encounter increased close-to-home reactivity, extreme misery, and a feeling of profound deadness. Feeling

guideline systems might be compromised, affecting, generally speaking, prosperity.

3. Confidence and self-esteem:
Discouragement frequently disintegrates confidence and self-esteem. Pessimistic self-discernments add to an inescapable insecurity and uselessness, increasing the close-to-home weight of the condition.

4. Survival strategies:
The methodologies people use to adapt to life stressors can impact the turn of events and support melancholy. Maladaptive survival techniques, like evasion or rumination, may add to the steadiness of burdensome side effects.

5. Relational Connections:
Examples of cooperation in connections assume a huge part in wretchedness. Troubles in shaping and keeping up with significant associations, combined with difficulties in correspondence and social withdrawal, add to a feeling of disengagement.

6. Psychodynamic Variables:
Psychodynamic viewpoints investigate the impact of oblivious cycles on sorrow. Unsettled clashes, early educational encounters, and oblivious elements can shape the turn of events and the articulation of burdensome side effects.

7. Mental Conduct Variables:
Mental conduct models feature the learned ways of behaving and thought designs in despondency. Negative support cycles,

evasion ways of behaving, and maladaptive reasoning styles add to the upkeep of burdensome side effects.

8. Character Variables:
Certain character qualities are related to weakness and sadness. Characteristics like neuroticism, compulsiveness, and a propensity to incorporate stressors can add to the turn of events and compound burdensome side effects.

9. Stress and life-altering situations:
The effect of pressure and life-altering situations on psychological wellness is significant. Significant life-altering events, ongoing stressors, and horrible encounters can go about as triggers for sadness, impacting its beginning and course.

10. Existential and Significance-Making Aspects:
Inquiries about significance, reason, and existential worries can become unmistakable in the experience of wretchedness. People might wrestle with existential topics, like the quest for importance, notwithstanding their languishing

Understanding the mental elements of wretchedness includes investigating the multifaceted connections between contemplations, feelings, ways of behaving, and relational elements. Mediations focusing on these mental aspects, like psychotherapy and mental conduct draws, are instrumental in tending to the intricacies of despondency and encouraging a long way towards recuperating.

Environmental Influences on Depression: Navigating the External Terrain

Past natural and mental aspects, the outside climate assumes a huge part in molding the course of depression. Different natural elements can add to the beginning, compounding, or mitigation of burdensome side effects, highlighting the significance of a comprehensive comprehension.

1. Early valuable encounters:
Adolescent encounters, including injury, disregard, or antagonistic occasions, can lastingly affect emotional wellness. Early life stressors might expand weakness to depression further down the road.

2. Socially and emotionally supportive networks:
The presence or nonattendance of steady informal communities is a basic natural component. Solid social help can go about as a defensive cradle, while social disengagement and the absence of steady connections can add to the turn of events or the tirelessness of melancholy.

3. Life Stressors and Difficulties:
Persistent stressors, significant life-altering events, and continuous misfortunes can fundamentally influence emotional wellness. Natural stressors, for example, monetary troubles, relationship issues, or business-related difficulties, may add to the beginning of burdensome side effects.

4. Social and Cultural Impacts:

Shawdow inside

Social and cultural elements shape the experience of sorrow. Belittling of psychological wellness, cultural perspectives toward looking for help, and social standards around profound articulation can impact how people see and adapt to despondency.

5. Admittance to Medical Care and Emotional Well-Being Administrations:

Variations in admission to medical care and emotional wellness administrations can influence the course of wretchedness. Restricted admittance might defer determination and treatment, intensifying the burdensome side effects.

6. Monetary Variables:

Financial precariousness and financial status can contribute to the advancement of wretchedness. Monetary pressure, joblessness, and the absence of assets might enhance the weight of emotional well-being difficulties.

7. Actual climate:

Actual environmental factors, including everyday environments and openness to natural stressors, can impact mental prosperity. Factors, for example, lodging shakiness or openness to contamination, might add to the turn of events or worsen the despondency.

8. Instructive Encounters:

Instructive conditions and encounters can influence emotional well-being. Scholastic tensions, harassment, or challenges in the school system might contribute to the advancement of burdensome side effects, especially in more youthful people.

9. Media and Innovation:
The unavoidable impact of media and innovation can shape insights and add to pressure. Extreme openness to negative substances, cyberbullying, or the effect of virtual entertainment on confidence can be ecological elements impacting discouragement.

10. Life Advances:
Critical life advances, like marriage, being a parent, or retirement, can influence emotional well-being. Acclimating to significant life-altering events might add pressure and impact the beginning or course of burdensome side effects.

Understanding and tending to ecological impacts includes perceiving the interconnectedness of individual encounters with more extensive cultural, social, and monetary elements. Thorough intercessions for misery frequently think about these ecological elements, planning to make strong and enabling settings for people exploring the intricacies of emotional well-being difficulties.

Section 4

Voices from the Abyss: Echoes of Silent Struggles

In the huge breadth of human life, there exists a profundity only sometimes investigated—the void where quiet battles unfurl, disguised behind the façade of daily existence. "Shadows Inside: Exploring the Deepness of Depression" entices us to pay attention to the voices arising out of this void, to intensify the accounts of the people who have confronted sadness and gotten comfortable with themselves in the midst of the quietude of inside strife.
Individual stories are the strings that line together the texture of figuring things out, winding around an embroidery of shared encounters. In this part, we listen attentively to the tales of people who have navigated the maze of sadness. These stories are not simple records; they are reverberations from the pit, resounding with the intricacy, torment, and strength that portray the quiet battles inside.

The primary murmur from the pit might be a story of introductory disarray—a vulnerability about the changing tints of feeling, a battle to unravel the language of the psyche. It is a story of acknowledgment, of finding some peace with an undetectable foe that creates an inescapable shaded area. Through these accounts, we recognize the mental fortitude it takes to stand up to the obscure inside oneself.

Shawdow inside

As we adventure further, we experience stories that reverberate the seclusion that frequently goes with melancholy. The void can be a forlorn spot where the reverberation of one's own considerations resounds, muffling the hints of association. These accounts advise us that a downturn isn't just a fight with oneself but an excursion that frequently unfurls in isolation. However, inside this isolation, there is a significant longing for understanding and sympathy.

The voices from the pit additionally discuss flexibility—the solidarity to endure the tempests and fury inside. They share the systems conceived to explore the dimness, the snapshots of win anyway little, and the examples learned through misfortune. These stories are encouraging signs, enlightening the chance of arising out of the profundities and advising us that the human soul has an inborn limit with regards to recharging.

In "Shadows Inside," these voices are not simple repeats yet basic parts of the account. By enhancing these accounts, we aim to overcome any issues of seclusion and association. Through shared encounters, we desire to destroy the walls that frequently bind those wrestling with sorrow, cultivating an aggregate comprehension that rises above the limits of individual battles.

As we drench ourselves in the voices from the void, let us remember that these stories are not confined stories but rather strings in the more extensive embroidery of the human experience. They advise us that, in recognizing and regarding these voices, we add to the aggregate story of flexibility,

Shawdow inside

sympathy, and perseverance through the human limit with respect to development in the midst of the shadows.

Personal Narratives: Illuminating the Human Experience of Depression

Inside the perplexing embroidered artwork of sadness, individual accounts arise as strong strings, winding together individual accounts of battle, flexibility, and development. These stories give a significant comprehension of the human experience, rising above the clinical focal point and offering understanding into the one-of-a kind excursions of those contacted by sadness.

1. Quiet Battles Uncovered:
Individual stories uncover the quiet battles that frequently slip by everyone's notice. Through sincere records, people share the profundity of their inner strife, offering a brief look into the interior fights pursued inside the domain of despondency.

2. Exploring Shadows:
These accounts explore the shadows of depression, chronicling the difficulties of day-to-day existence under the heaviness of burdensome side effects. From the least complex errands to significant choices, individual stories delineate the nuanced effect of depression on each aspect of presence.

3. Snapshots of Sadness:
Inside private accounts, snapshots of hopelessness are uncovered. People portray the significant forlornness, sadness,

and grasping feeling of dimness that describe the profundities of burdensome episodes.

4. Versatility and Win:

Entwined with stories of battle are accounts of flexibility and victory. Individual stories enlighten the strength that rises up out of the shadows, exhibiting the limit of people's ability to explore misfortune, look for help, and produce a way toward mending.

5. Looking for Association:

Individual stories frequently uncover a profound longing for association. People share their experiences of connecting, whether through looking for proficient assistance, trusting in friends and family, or associating with steady networks. These accounts highlight the significance of human association in the excursion through discouragement.

6. The Effect on Connections:

Inside private stories, the effect of melancholy on connections is investigated. People think about how their psychological well-being difficulties impact associations with family, companions, and better halves, giving bits of knowledge into the intricate interaction among sorrow and social elements.

7. A Kaleidoscope of Feelings:

Individual stories paint a kaleidoscope of feelings. From the profundities of distress to short-lived snapshots of delight, these accounts capture the close-to-home intricacy inborn in the experience of sadness. They challenge generalizations and feature the nuanced close-to-home scene that people explore.

8. Reflections on Recuperation:
Stories of recuperation offer a look at trust and recharging. People share the methodologies, intercessions, and snapshots of self-revelation that add to their recuperation. These accounts rouse others on comparative excursions and show that recuperation is a multi-layered, progressing process.

9. Ending Quietness:
Maybe in particular, individual accounts end the quiet, encompassing despondency. By sharing their accounts, people contribute to destigmatizing psychological wellness, cultivating understanding, and making a space for open exchange about the difficulties and wins inborn in the excursion through misery.

In the mosaic of individual stories, an aggregate story of versatility, boldness, and the quest for prosperity arises. These accounts highlight the significance of recognizing and esteeming the different encounters of those impacted by sadness, underscoring that inside every story lies the potential for association, compassion, and common perspective.

Breaking the Silence: Shattering Stigmas Surrounding Depression

Ending the quiet-encompassing depression is a valiant demonstration that destroys hindrances, encourages understanding, and develops a climate where people feel seen, heard, and upheld. This is the way the aggregate work to end

Shawdow inside

the quiet adds to reshaping the account around emotional wellness:

1. Destigmatizing Emotional wellness:
Ending the quietness is a critical stage in destigmatizing psychological wellness. By straightforwardly examining despondency, people challenge generalizations and confusions, advancing a culture that sees emotional wellness challenges with sympathy instead of judgment.

2. Encouraging Sympathy and Understanding:
Individual stories and open discussions cultivate sympathy and understanding. Ending the quietness permits others to observe the complex profound scene of melancholy, advancing a more profound cognizance of the difficulties people face.

3. Empowering Help-Chasing Conduct:
At the point when the quiet is broken, it sends a strong message that looking for help is certainly not an indication of shortcomings however a gallant move toward mending. Empowering help-chasing conduct becomes fundamental in reshaping the account around psychological well-being.

4. Making Strong People group:
The open exchange about depression creates a feeling of the local area where people have a good sense of security to share their encounters. Ending the quiet sustains strong conditions that recognize the legitimacy of every individual's excursion.

5. Approving Individual Encounters:

Shawdow inside

Ending the quietness approves the different encounters of those contacted by sorrow. It recognizes that every story is remarkable, dissipating the idea of a one-size-fits-all way to deal with emotional well-being.

6. Enabling People:
Sharing individual stories enables people to recover their accounts. It moves the account from one of disgrace to one of versatility, representing that people are not characterized by their psychological well-being difficulties.

7. Rousing Others to Stand up:
At the point when one individual ends the quietness, it frequently motivates others to do likewise. This aggregate exertion has a far-reaching influence, bit by bit changing cultural perspectives and standards encompassing emotional wellness.

8. Featuring the Human Association:
The demonstration of ending the quiet underlines the widespread idea of human battles. It features that psychological well-being difficulties, including sadness, are essential for the common human experience, cultivating association and a feeling of solidarity.

9. Upholding for Fundamental Change:
Open discussions about discouragement add to support endeavors for foundational change. Ending the quiet prompts conversations about the significance of emotional well-being in different circles, including medical services, training, and work environments.

10. Advancing Avoidance and Early Mediation:
By transparently talking about wretchedness, the center can move towards anticipation and early intercession. Ending the quiet supports mindfulness, training, and proactive measures to address psychological well-being difficulties before they arise.

Ending the quietness is certainly not a solitary demonstration however an aggregate undertaking that includes people, networks, and social orders. As the quiet breaks, it prepares for a more merciful, understanding, and comprehensive way to deal with psychological wellness — one that perceives the strength in weakness and the force of shared stories to achieve positive change.

Section 5

Ways Through the Darkness: Illuminating Paths of Resilience

In the maze of wretchedness, where shadows develop and feelings falter, the mission for light becomes central. "Shadows Inside: Exploring the Deepness of Depression" welcomes us to investigate the different ways that wind through the obscurity, offering encouraging signs, flexibility, and change. In this section, we enlighten the course through the haziness, recognizing that inside the multifaceted woven artwork of melancholy, there are strings of solidarity ready to be found.

Methods for dealing with hardship or stress:
The excursion through misery frequently requires the advancement of survival techniques—systems to explore the profound territory. These are the devices people produce to deal with obscurity directly. From care rehearses that focus on the current second to innovative articulations that give an outlet to feelings, survival strategies become lights that aid through the maze.

Restorative Methodologies:
Proficient direction and restorative intercessions stand as mainstays of help along the way. "Shadows Inside" investigates the different remedial methodologies—from mental social treatments that address misshaped thought examples to psychoanalytic methodologies digging into the

profundities of oblivious cycles. Through these helpful roads, people track down friendship in prepared experts, offering experiences and direction toward mending.

Ways of life change:
Once in a while, the manner in which the haziness occurs includes reshaping the outer scene. Way of life changes encompass modifications in everyday schedules, consolidating exercise, a reasonable eating regimen, and sufficient rest. These progressions are about actual wellbeing as well as the unpredictable association between the body and the brain, encouraging a comprehensive way to deal with prosperity.

In this part, we perceive that these courses through the dimness are not one-size-fits-all arrangements. The excursion is private, and people explore it as indicated by their exceptional assets and conditions. The investigation of survival strategies, remedial methodologies, and way of life changes turns into a guide, not an inflexible aide, considering adaptability and variation to the steadily moving forms of the profound scene.

As we dig into the routes through the obscurity, we observe that these ways are not direct. They might circle back, meet, or wander, reflecting the intricacy of the human experience. Every way is a demonstration of versatility, a stage taken notwithstanding difficulty, and a pledge to track down the light in the midst of the shadows.

Shawdow inside

"Shadows Inside" stretches out a challenge to ponder these courses through the dimness, understanding that they are not just systems but rather accounts of boldness and constancy. Through the investigation of these ways, we desire to move those wrestling with sorrow to find their own wellsprings of solidarity, understanding that inside the obscurity, there exists the potential for significant change and restoration.

Standing Up to Disgrace: Dissipating Legends and Encouraging Comprehension

In the scene of emotional wellness, disgrace looms as a considerable boundary, creating shaded areas that darken comprehension and sympathy. "Shadows Inside: Exploring the Deepness of Depression" welcomes us to face this shame, to unwind the fantasies that cover wretchedness, and to cultivate a climate of sympathy and acknowledgment.

Fantasies and Confusions:
Shame frequently emerges from profoundly imbued legends and confusions encompassing emotional well-being, propagating generalizations that prevent open talk. "Shadows Inside" dives into these fantasies, presenting them to the illumination of examination. From the idea that a downturn is a simple close-to-home shortcoming to the misinterpretation that it is a transient stage that effectively survives, every fantasy is taken apart to uncover the nuanced reality underneath.

Shawdow inside

The Language of Understanding:
Standing up to disgrace isn't just about dispersing misrepresentations; it is tied in with developing a language of understanding. This part investigates the force of words and accounts in forming judgments. By recognizing the effect of language on emotional wellness talk, "Shadows Inside" tries to reclassify the discussion around misery. It underscores the significance of picking words that enable instead of demonize, cultivating a shared mindset that perceives the legitimacy of every individual's battle.

The Job of Training:
Schooling turns into a critical weapon in the fight against shame. "Shadows Inside" advocates for broad psychological well-being proficiency, encouraging schools, working environments, and networks to focus on instruction on discouragement and related conditions. By giving exact data, cultivating compassion, and advancing open exchange, training turns into an impetus for destroying the obstructions of misconception that propagate disgrace.

As we face shame, it becomes obvious that this is definitely not a solitary exertion but an aggregate undertaking. People, groups, and establishments should join to challenge the generalizations that cast shadows over those managing discouragement. By sharing stories, scattering fantasies, and cultivating a culture of transparency, "Shadows Inside" imagines an existence where emotional well-being is drawn closer with a similar comprehension and sympathy as actual wellbeing.

Shawdow inside

The showdown of shame is an indispensable piece of the excursion through the profundities of discouragement. It is a source of inspiration, an encouragement to reshape cultural perspectives, and a guarantee to create a space where people feel seen, heard, and comprehended. In "Shadows Inside," standing up to disgrace isn't simply a section; it is a statement for change, an announcement that the shadows cast by shame can be scattered by the aggregate light of mindfulness, sympathy, and training.

Section 6

Anchors in the Storm: The Role of Relationships in Depression

In the whirlwind of depression, where feelings twirl and shadows extend, connections arise as anchors, giving dependability, support, and help through the tempest. "Shadows Inside: Exploring the Deepness of Depression" devotes a section to investigating the significant role job connections play in the excursion through melancholy, remembering them as signals that guide people toward trust and mending.

The Isolation of Depression:
Depression frequently projects people into significant isolation, separating them from the world and, once in a while, even from those nearest to them. In this part, we dive into the subtleties of this isolation, recognizing the difficulties it poses to both the individual encountering despondency and the connections that encompass them. It becomes obvious that exploring the tempest requires a comprehension of the intricacies that emerge when isolation and association converge.

Association as a Wellspring of Solace:
In the midst of the shadows, associations with companions, family, and accomplices become wellsprings of solace and understanding. "Shadows Inside" investigates the force of compassionate tuning in, unrestricted help, and the

Shawdow inside

straightforward demonstrations of friendship that can act as life savers for people wrestling with melancholy. These associations act as anchors, establishing people amidst close-to-home disturbances.

Building a Steady People Group:
Past individual connections, the part dives into the more extensive idea of local area support. Whether through help gatherings, online discussions, or grassroots drives, fabricating a strong local area turns into a fundamental part of exploring the deepness of depression. The common encounters inside these networks give a feeling of having a place, scattering the separation that frequently goes with psychological well-being difficulties.

The Effect on Connections:
The excursion through misery isn't exclusively about the individual; it additionally leaves an engraving on connections. "Shadows Inside" investigates the unique transaction among discouragement and connections, tending to the strain it might put on associations. It underlines the significance of open correspondence, common comprehension, and the job of tolerance in supporting connections through the difficulties of psychological well-being battles.

As we explore the section on "Anchors in the Tempest," it becomes clear that connections are not uninvolved observers but rather dynamic members in the excursion through depression. They offer basic encouragement as well as act as observers of the developing story of strength and recuperation. Through stories and reflections, "Shadows

Shawdow inside

Inside" plans to enlighten the complicated dance among people and their anchors, featuring the extraordinary force of association despite difficulty.

In this investigation, we recognize that connections are not a panacea, nor are they resistant to the intricacies of psychological wellness challenges. Be that as it may, by understanding their importance and cultivating a culture of help, we endeavor to make a story where the shadows of misery are mellowed by the glow of human association and where secures in the tempest become directing lights toward a more brilliant tomorrow.

Section 7

Rays of Resilience: Stories of Triumph Amidst the Shadows

In the perplexing woven artwork of depression, where shadows loom and feelings overflow, there exist stories that enlighten the story with beams of flexibility. "Shadows Inside: Exploring the Deepness of Depression" gives a section to these accounts—confirmations of win, strength, and the unstoppable human soul that sparkles even in the most obscure of times.

Accounts of Win:
This part is a festival of individual stories, each an exceptional excursion through the maze of sorrow. By sharing accounts of victories, "Shadows Inside" plans to end the quiet encompassing emotional well-being difficulties, uncovering that inside the battle lies the potential for development, self-revelation, and versatility. These accounts become encouraging signs, offering motivation to those exploring their own ways through the shadows.

Little Triumphs and Ordinary Versatility:
Strength is in many cases tracked down in the little triumphs—the snapshots of mental fortitude, the means taken toward mending, and the everyday endeavors to confront the difficulties of despondency. "Shadows Inside" investigates the idea of regular flexibility, perceiving that winning isn't generally pompous but can be tracked down in the versatility

Shawdow inside

to confront one more day, to look for help, or to participate in taking care of oneself.

Illustrations from Affliction:
Difficulty, while imposing, likewise harbors examples. This part dives into the extraordinary force of affliction, recognizing that the shadows of sorrow can become cauldrons for self-improvement. It investigates how people, through their flexibility, gather shrewdness and knowledge that rise above prompt difficulties, molding a more significant comprehension of themselves and others.

The Aggregate Flexibility of Networks:
Past individual stories, "Shadows Inside" likewise examines the aggregate versatility of networks. Whether through grassroots developments, encouraging groups of people, or social movements, networks can play an urgent part in cultivating versatility. By enhancing accounts of aggregate flexibility, this section underlines the interconnectedness of individual battles and the potential for public help in exploring the deepness of depression.

In investigating the beams of versatility, it becomes clear that victory over depression is certainly not a straight excursion. It includes misfortunes, curves, and turns, yet inside these intricacies, versatility arises as a directing power. By recognizing and praising flexibility, "Shadows Inside" looks to reclassify the account encompassing sorrow, stressing that it isn't just an account of battle but also one of win, development, and the resolute strength of the human soul.

Shawdow inside

As we dive into these stories, may they act as a wellspring of motivation, consolation, and certification. Through the sharing of stories, "Shadows Inside" tries to create a space where versatility isn't just perceived but celebrated—a demonstration of the perseverance through strength that can rise out of the shadows and enlighten the way toward a more brilliant, stronger future.

Section 8

The Path to Recovery: Navigating Towards Healing

In the maze of depression, the way to recuperation wanders through shadows and light, an excursion set apart by strength, self-disclosure, and the quest for prosperity. "Shadows Inside: Exploring the Deepness of Depression" commits a part to investigating this critical stage, recognizing that recuperation isn't an objective yet a nonstop, developing interaction.

Looking for Proficient Assistance:
The excursion toward recuperation frequently starts with the vital stage of looking for proficient help. This part underlines the significance of emotional well-being experts—advisors, instructors, and specialists—who act as guides through the complexities of wretchedness. "Shadows Inside" perceives that expert assistance is certainly not an indication of shortcoming, yet a fearless decision, offering custom-made systems and backing.

A Comprehensive Methodology:
Recuperation isn't bound to the psyche alone; it reaches out to the body and soul. This part digs into the idea of a comprehensive way to deal with mending, where actual prosperity, psychological well-being, and profound satisfaction are interconnected. "Shadows Inside" investigates practices like care, exercise, and self-reflection as vital parts of a thorough recuperation technique.

Shawdow inside

Figuring out Backslides and Mishaps:
Exploring the way to recuperation is frequently accompanied
by snapshots of progress and difficulties. This section tends to
the truth of backslides; it isn't generally direct to recognize
that the excursion Understanding and gaining from difficulties
become fundamental components of the recuperation cycle,
underscoring strength and the ability to adjust despite
difficulties.

Building an encouraging group of people:
Recuperation is definitely not a singular undertaking.
Fabricating and keeping a powerful, encouraging group of
people is investigated in this part, perceiving the job of
companions, family, and the local area in giving support and
understanding. "Shadows Inside" stresses that a strong climate
cultivates flexibility, making an establishment for supported
prosperity.

Embracing Self-Empathy:
Integral to the process of recuperation is the development of
self-empathy. This part digs into the significance of treating
oneself with consideration, recognizing that recuperating
includes tending to difficulties as well as cultivating a positive
relationship with oneself. "Shadows Inside" urges people to
embrace self-empathy as a core value on the journey to
recuperation.

As we investigate the way to recuperate, it becomes clear that
it is a profoundly private and one-of-a kind excursion for
every person. "Shadows Inside" underlines that recuperation

Shawdow inside

is definitely not a direct walk towards a proper endpoint; rather, it is a continuous cycle set apart by self-revelation, flexibility, and the quest for a satisfying and healthy lifestyle. May this part act as an aide, a wellspring of consolation, and an update that recuperation isn't just imaginable yet an insistence of one's solidarity and limit with respect to development. In recognizing the intricacies of the way to recuperation, "Shadows Inside" looks to enlighten the way forward, offering backing and understanding to those exploring the difficult yet extraordinary territory of mending from despondency.

Section 9

Cultivating Mental Well-being: Nurturing the Garden Within

In the orchestra of life, mental prosperity is the agreeable harmony that resounds through our viewpoints, feelings, and activities. "Shadows Inside: Exploring the Deepness of Depression" closes its investigation with a section committed to developing mental prosperity—a comprehensive undertaking that encompasses taking care of oneself, positive propensities, and a careful way to deal with life.

Taking care of oneself Methodologies:
At the core of mental prosperity lies the act of taking care of oneself, a purposeful and empathetic obligation to support one's physical, personal, and psychological well-being. This part investigates assorted ways of taking care of oneself, from straightforward everyday customs to vivid exercises that renew the spirit. "Shadows Inside" stresses that taking care of oneself isn't an extravagance yet a central part of keeping up with mental prosperity.

Careful Living:
Care turns into a core value in the development of mental prosperity. This section dives into the groundbreaking force of living right now, encouraging mindfulness, and embracing acknowledgment. Careful practices, like contemplation and careful breathing, are investigated as instruments to explore

Shawdow inside

the intricacies of the brain and advance a feeling of quiet in the midst of life's tempests.

Forestalling Repeat:
As people rise out of the shadows of melancholy, preventing the repetition of burdensome episodes becomes a crucial thought. "Shadows Inside" inspects the systems and way of life decisions that contribute to long-term mental prosperity. It underscores the significance of building versatility, perceiving triggers, and carrying out precautionary estimates in the continuous excursion towards wellbeing.

The Job of Positive Connections:
Developing mental prosperity stretches beyond private practices to the nature of the connections that encompass us. This section investigates the advantageous connection between certain associations and emotional well-being. "Shadows Inside" highlights the meaning of cultivating sound connections, as they contribute not exclusively to individual prosperity but additionally make a steady organization that goes about as a support against life's difficulties.

A Comprehensive Methodology:
The development of mental prosperity is definitely not a one-size-fits-all undertaking. This section advocates for an all-encompassing methodology that thinks about the interconnectedness of different parts of life—actual wellbeing, close-to-home flexibility, social associations, and a feeling of direction. "Shadows Inside" perceives that an all-encompassing viewpoint cultivates a more far-reaching and getting-through condition of prosperity.

Shawdow inside

In finishing up the excursion through "Shadows Inside," the section on developing mental prosperity fills in as both a reflection and an aide. It perceives that psychological prosperity is certainly not a proper objective yet a persistent course of watching out for the nursery inside—a nursery that, when sustained with care, blossoms with strength, inspiration, and a significant identity.

May this part be an asset, offering bits of knowledge, motivation, and useful direction for those looking to develop and keep up with their psychological prosperity. In recognizing the intricacies of this excursion, "Shadows Inside" confirms the limit inside every person to keep an eye on their inward nursery, encouraging a dynamic and prospering scene of emotional well-being.

Taking Care of Yourself Techniques: Sustaining Your Prosperity

In the ensemble of life, taking care of oneself is the delicate song that reverberates through our everyday mood, sustaining our physical, close-to-home, and mental prosperity. As we dive into taking care of oneself techniques inside the setting of "Shadows Inside: Exploring the Deepness of Depression," we should investigate purposeful practices that act as anchors in the tempest of difficulties.

1. Careful Breathing and Contemplation:

Shawdow inside

Start by embracing the straightforwardness of careful relaxation. Breathe in quietness; breathe out strain. Investigate contemplation as a device to calm the brain, cultivating a feeling of quiet in the midst of the tempest of considerations.

2. Laying out an everyday practice:
Structure gives a feeling of security. Make a day-to-day schedule that incorporates customary rest examples, dinners, and minutes for unwinding. Consistency turns into a soothing anchor in eccentric times.

3. Participating in active work:
Practice is a strong partner in advancing both physical and mental prosperity. Whether it's a lively walk, yoga, or a dance meeting, find a movement that gives pleasure and gets your body rolling.

4. Developing Solid Rest Propensities:
Rest is the foundation of prosperity. Focus on a tranquil night by laying out a quiet sleep schedule, establishing an agreeable rest climate, and going for the gold examples.

5. Feeding Sustenance:
Fuel your body with nutritious food sources that contribute to your overall well-being. Investigate a diet rich in natural products, vegetables, lean proteins, and whole grains. Hydration is similarly crucial for keeping up with ideal prosperity.

6. Defining Limits:

Shawdow inside

Figure out how to say no when required and define limits to safeguard your psychological and close-to-home space. Laying out limits is definitely not an indication of a shortcoming but rather a demonstration of taking care of oneself and protecting your energy for the main thing.

7. Rehearsing Appreciation:
Think back on the good aspects of your life to cultivate an appreciation habit. Journaling, or basically recognizing snapshots of appreciation, can move your concentration from difficulties to wellsprings of happiness.

8. Associating with Nature:
Nature soothingly affects the psyche. Take minutes to associate with the outside, whether it's a stroll in the park, sitting by a waterway, or just valuing the excellence of the normal world.

9. Inventive Articulation:
Participate in exercises that consider imaginative articulation. Whether it's craft, composing, music, or any type of self-articulation, innovativeness turns into a helpful source for feelings.

10. Social Association:
Focus on time with strong loved ones. Significant social associations give a feeling of having a place and contribute to close-to-home prosperity. Plan standard connections, regardless of whether they are virtual.

Shawdow inside

Keep in mind that taking care of oneself is certainly not a one-size-fits-all methodology. Investigate and customize these methodologies to accommodate your exceptional necessities. As you explore the profundities of "Shadows Inside," may these taking care of oneself practices be the compass directing you toward a position of equilibrium, flexibility, and supported prosperity.

Conclusion:

As we arrive at the end of "Shadows Inside: Exploring the Deepness of Depression," we wind up at a point that marks both an end and a start. This investigation into the perplexing scene of sadness has not been a simple entry through murkiness; it has been an excursion of figuring out, empathy, and the acknowledgment that inside the shadows, there exists the potential for significant change.

The pages of this story have unfurled to uncover the diverse idea of sadness—from its quiet beginning to the intricate embroidered artwork of organic, mental, and ecological elements. We have paid attention to the voices from the pit, enhancing the stories of quiet battles that frequently slip through the cracks. In exploring the courses through the murkiness, we have found survival strategies, remedial methodologies, and the significance of way of life changes.

Standing up to disgrace turned into a call to scatter fantasies and cultivate understanding, perceiving that an aggregate change in cultural mentalities is fundamental for establishing a more compassionate and comprehensive climate. Secures in the tempest featured the urgent job connections play in offering help and figuring out, going about as reference points through the profound choppiness.

Beams of versatility enlightened the account with accounts of win, showing that even inside the shadows, people track down strength, development, and the limit with regards to reestablishment. The way to recuperation arose as a ceaseless,

Shawdow inside

developing excursion, set apart by looking for proficient
assistance, embracing an all-encompassing methodology, and
grasping the subtleties of misfortunes and progress.
In developing mental prosperity, we investigated the practices
and systems that add to a decent and satisfying life, perceiving
that taking care of oneself, care, and positive connections
structure the groundwork of enduring emotional well-being.

Presently, as we finish up this investigation, it is fundamental
to recognize that the excursion through wretchedness is
certainly not a direct story with a conveniently tied closure.
All things considered, it is a consistently advancing story,
with turns, turns, and surprising parts. The determination is
certainly not a last objective, but a progress to the following
period of the excursion—a stage set apart by continuous self-
disclosure, flexibility, and the quest for a day-to-day existence
that reverberates with prosperity.

For the people who have strolled close by these pages, may
the experiences acquired act as partners on your own
excursion. For those who are now exploring the shadows of
sorrow, may this investigation offer a brief look at trust,
understanding, and the acknowledgment that you are in good
company.

"Shadows Inside" finishes up not with conclusiveness but
rather with a greeting—to proceed with the discussion, to
encourage compassion and mindfulness, and to add to a
reality where psychological well-being is perceived,
acknowledged, and focused on. As we embrace the steadily
advancing excursion, may it be directed by sympathy,

Shawdow inside

versatility, and the faithful conviction that inside the shadows, there is consistently the potential for light.
Embrace Trust: A Directing Light in the Shadows

In the embroidery of life, trust arises as a glowing string, winding through the intricacies of our encounters. As we close the excursion through "Shadows Inside: Exploring the Deepness of Depression," embracing trust as both an insistence and a directing light in the midst of the shadows is principal.

A Signal in the Haziness:
Trust is the immovable conviction that, even in the haziest minutes, there exists the potential for light. It fills in as a guide, slicing through the shadows of sadness and offering a brief look at potential outcomes beyond the ongoing battles. This part energizes the affirmation of trust as well as its dynamic hug as a strong power for change.

The Versatility of Trust:
Even with difficulty, trust uncovers its strength. It's anything but a detached observer, however, a functioning member of the excursion through depression. "Shadows Inside" investigates accounts of win, versatility, and the extraordinary force of trust. These accounts act as demonstrations of the getting-through soul that can rise out of the profundities of depression.

Developing Expectations in Day-to-Day Existence:
Embracing trust isn't restricted to excellent motions; it unfurls in the subtleties of regular day-to-day existence. This part

Shawdow inside

energizes the development of trust through little, purposeful activities—whether it be laying out reasonable objectives, rehearsing appreciation, or taking part in exercises that give pleasure. It highlights that trust is certainly not a theoretical idea but rather a living presence that can be supported.

Shared Trust:
As we explore the intricacies of emotional wellness, it becomes clear that trust is certainly not a singular undertaking. Shared trust is an aggregate strength that rises above individual battles. "Shadows Inside" underscores the significance of encouraging a culture where trust isn't just embraced independently but also shared mutually, establishing a strong climate that supports prosperity.

The Consistently Advancing Excursion of Trust:
The end of "Shadows Inside" isn't a goodbye to trust; all things considered, it denotes a change to a steadily developing excursion directed by trust. It perceives that trust is certainly not a static objective yet a powerful power that develops with each step taken. This part urges people to convey trust as a steady friend, enlightening the way ahead.

In embracing trust, we certify the flexibility of the human soul, the limit with regards to development, and the chance of a more splendid tomorrow. As we finish up this investigation, it may be a closing note as well as an introduction to fresh starts—a persevering through presence that goes with every person on their exceptional excursion through the unpredictable scenes of life.

Shawdow inside

"Shadows Inside" says goodbye with the challenge to convey trust forward, perceiving that inside its hug, there exists the extraordinary ability to explore the shadows and arise into the glow of a confident and satisfying future.

www.ingramcontent.com/pod-product-compliance
Lightning Source LLC
Chambersburg PA
CBHW071104260726
48661CB00006B/2459